Antonio Cuyás

Text of the new Reform Measure for the Island of Cuba

Antonio Cuyás

Text of the new Reform Measure for the Island of Cuba

ISBN/EAN: 9783337228422

Printed in Europe, USA, Canada, Australia, Japan

Cover: Foto ©ninafisch / pixelio.de

More available books at **www.hansebooks.com**

TEXT

OF THE

NEW REFORM MEASURE

FOR THE

ISLAND OF CUBA.

"EXPOSITORY PREAMBLE" AND "ROYAL DECREE."

COMMENTARY—STATEMENTS BY PUBLIC
MEN—EXPRESSIONS OF OPINION.

ENGLISH VERSION BY

ANTONIO CUYÁS.

NEW YORK:
PUBLISHED BY THE ASSOCIATED SPANISH AND CUBAN PRESS.
1897.

EXPOSITORY PREAMBLE.

YOUR MAJESTY: Ever since Your Majesty's confidence was reposed in the present Ministry the war in Cuba has been the object of its constant anxiety, which was later heightened by the rebellion in the Philippine Archipelago. To-day the end of the latter seems to be near; and although no precise date can be predetermined for the ending of the Cuban insurrection, its evident abatement suffices to warrant certain measures in anticipation of and adequate to the probable course of events.

It is important, Your Majesty, that the facts anteceding these events be borne in mind. It is daily becoming more evident that the protracted conspiracy which preceded the war was not entered into with the end in view of obtaining any concessions compatible with Spanish sovereignty, as there exists ample documentary evidence to prove that the promoters of said conspiracy never contemplated anything but the independence of the Island. So manifestly was this their aim that, as is well known, the Reform Law of March 15, 1895, which was supported in the Cortes with such good faith by all political parties, Peninsular and Cuban, far from restraining the revolutionary movement, hastened its outbreak, it being the purpose of the conspirators to prevent the beneficial effects of said law from exerting any direct or indirect influence toward the maintenance of peace. Thus, forcibly, the Spanish nation, which had long before granted to its Antilles all the political rights unanimously accepted by modern civilization, and which, at the very time when its sovereignty began to be combatted, was endeavoring to establish certain reform measures, indisputably liberal and in the direction of self-government, was obliged to take up arms in defence of the integrity of its territory. Some persons were led by their generous spirit to believe at first that by merely putting the reforms into practical operation the plans of the conspirators would be baffled; but the majority of Spaniards soon became convinced that we had to deal with another separatist war, the inefficiency of which would have to be demonstrated before the concessions contained in the Reform Law could give any useful results. To this conviction and to the manifest impossibility—soon afterward created by the war—of introducing a new régime in Cuba, when the established one could barely be enforced, was due the postponement in putting the reforms into effect; a postponement which was not voluntary, therefore, but unavoidable. And since the settlement of the matter was intrusted to the force of arms, not through choice of the mother country, but much against her wishes, it has been necessary for us to wait until arms should determine the precise moment in which to employ other means dictated by reason and justice.

Of course the Reform Law, which had been approved by the Cortes (Congress), was never to be considered a finality in an evolution initiated by the metropolis with so much forethought and such sincerity. The doubt might have been entertained at one time whether it would have been advantageous even to the residents of the Antilles for them to enter suddenly on an autonomic form of government, in view of the ill effects of precipitate action in such matters.

Without going further than Cuba, we see that such ill effects had already been experienced in the matter of the sudden and unlimited freedom of the press, which was so largely instrumental in bringing about the insurrection.

All this notwithstanding, what Spanish or foreign statesman could suppose that where such liberal political rights existed, the mother country would be niggardly in granting administrative reforms to work in harmony with the political laws? No, it could not in good faith be assumed that the Reform Law of March 15, 1895, was a finality. It is evident, on the contrary, that the only limit not to be exceeded in the granting of concessions could and should be no other than that pointed out to Your Majesty's Government by the inexorable duty of preserving the nation's heritage.

But, as has been seen, to destroy the latter without any regard whatsoever to Spain's historical rights in the premises has been the chief intent of the rebels. They purposely ignored all peaceful means whereby they could, while in the free exercise of political rights, establish an administrative autonomy on solid bases. Instead of that they pandered to the impatient longings of the youth of the land; they excited the most anarchical passions; they denied all value to the advantages already acquired; they fostered the most unconquerable pessimism on the one hand, while on the other they aroused the most chimerical hopes. By such means they succeeded in having the above-mentioned law, which had been so enthusiastically passed by the Cortes, received both in Cuba and Porto Rico with indifference, if not with disdain, and in spreading the insurrectionary conflagration.

Some time has elapsed since those events. The war, with its manifold disasters, has been fruitful in severe lessons to all the well-disposed inhabitants of the Island of Cuba. Nor is it impossible that there should be a reawakening of the fraternal feeling so long dormant, but which among people of the same race can never be entirely extinguished; and certainly the persuasion that, after all, a peaceful and steady progress, though not satisfying every aspiration, is preferable to the triumphs of violence, no matter by whom obtained, is daily gaining ground.

Coincident with this there is evidently vanishing the mistaken opinion that Spain would be unable to carry on another war like the former one, an opinion held by those who, basing their judgment on insufficient data, attributed our magnanimity in Morocco to impotency, and who therefore thought that the struggle with the metropolis would be easy and of brief duration. The documents taken on various occasions from the insurgents prove conclusively that at one time even they were led into the same error, they who are our own brothers, and who therefore should never for a moment have doubted the firmness and virility of those of their race in the mother country.

In the meantime it is well known that, although Spain has been compelled, on account of the circumstances above recited, to postpone, and may be still obliged to defer, the carrying into effect of the liberal administrative régime that is essential to Cuba's future prosperity, she has never given up the intention of applying in due time the reforms approved by the Cortes, nor has she failed to appreciate the necessity of broadening their scope in such a manner as to satisfy both the Peninsulars and the Cubans who are shedding their blood on our side in the present struggle, as well as all the inabitants of the Island of Cuba who have the common welfare at heart. And the sincerity with which the new régime will be carried out by the home Government cannot, reasonably, even be questioned. To be convinced of this, we have but to remember the speech pronounced by Your Majesty on the occasion of the opening session of the present Cortes; for no one will doubt the loyalty of Your Majesty's Councilors, whosoever they may be, and, being loyal, it would be folly to assume that, whatever their differences of opinion on other matters, they would not all agree in upholding every Royal promise. No; such promises cannot ever be allowed to remain meaningless phrases, nor therefore shall those most solemn ones remain such, whereby Your Majesty offered to confer upon both the Antilles, as soon as the state of war would warrant it, "an administrative and economic personality of a purely local character, but which would assure the unimpeded intervention of all the people of the respective islands in their own affairs, while leaving the rights of sovereignty intact, and unimpaired the conditions necessary for their maintenance."

From that moment it was not to be questioned that any Spanish Government would shape its course to that end. In regard to the Ministry which is to-day favored with Your Majesty's confidence, it may be said that not only did its several members individually co-operate as efficiently as anyone else toward the approval of the aforementioned Reform Laws, but during the debate on the answer to the last speech from the Crown the present Cabinet, through its President (the Prime Minister), made certain statements which met with the approval of the most liberal of its political opponents, and which the Ministry could not, without jeopardy to its honor, fail to uphold.

One of the statements, Your Majesty, was to the effect that the Government would not wait until the last insurgent had disappeared from Cuba, but that it would deem the moment when the final victory should be assured and the national honor satisfied as the proper time to meet the real necessity felt in Cuba of testing what the English term "self-government," i. e., a liberal decentralization of such a nature as to allow the people of the Island to manage their own interests, and to assume, at the same time, the responsibility of their own acts, relieving the metropolis therefrom. Another of the statements made by the Prime Minister on the same occasion was that, aside from the serious motives hereinbefore mentioned, he was actuated to move, as he proposed moving, in regard to the policy for the West Indies, by a due consideration for the erroneous opinion prevailing in America and in Europe to the effect that we, the Peninsulars, obstinately denied to our brothers in Cuba and Porto Rico that which other nations granted their trans-oceanic provinces, an opinion which entailed upon us considerable injury. Such a notion was and is really most unjust, as is made evident by our colonial traditions and by our own conduct for many years past with regard to the political government of the West Indies. Notwithstanding this, it was not fitting that the Government should scorn this erroneous opinion, but, on the contrary, it deemed it a duty to dispel the causes thereof by practical measures. It never has, in truth, been advantageous for any one country to deviate in its political methods from the general trend of those of other nations, and the history of Spain amply bears out this assertion; and much less can it be advantageous at the present day, when the solidarity of all civilized peoples is such that a mere variance from the forms peculiar to the general system carried out by the predominant nations is usually fruitful of trouble. It is manifest that national dignity will always and in all countries spurn any measure that is not the expression of its own inmost conscience, spontaneously conceived, and much more will it spurn foreign imposition of any sort. But this does not imply that any power should systematically disregard public opinion, which, when legitimately expressed and generally held, is entitled to the same respect from the great human associations as from the individuals constituting them. In a word, Your Majesty, everything urges your Government to the fulfillment of the promises made by Your Majesty before the Cortes, and which by the Royal sanction, and with the consent of his colleagues, were repeated and extended in scope, also before the Cortes, by the Minister who has now the honor of addressing Your Majesty.

There is nothing, either, in what he submits for the Royal approval that is not in accord with his own political record. Before anyone else he devoted himself with energy and efficiency to the work of suppressing the slave trade; over thirty years ago he convened an important and illustrious assembly of delegates from the West Indies, intrusted with the task of thoroughly reforming in their respective provinces the then existing régime with regard to the administration of local affairs and to the labor question. After the capitulation of Zanjón he extended to Cuba, with such slight modifications as were at the beginning necessary, the exercise of the same political rights as were enjoyed in the Peninsula; and, lastly, as before mentioned, he contributed, together with all his political followers, without exception, toward the approval by the Cortes of the Reform Law of March, 1895. Such is the record to which the undersigned ventures to call the gracious attention of Your Majesty, not assuredly in a boastful spirit, but in order to strengthen the certitude which the natives of the West Indies should be possessed of that whatever Spain offers she stands ready to fulfill with inviolable good faith. For, if the present Prime Minister speaks now, more particularly in his own name, he hastens to acknowledge and proclaim that all other Councilors invested with Your Majesty's confidence will in the future act in like manner, because Spanish statesmen can differ in regard to this question only in their ability or in the degree of success they may attain, but never in their good faith or in their loyalty in redeeming the pledges made in Your Majesty's name and on behalf of the nation.

With the issuance of this Decree Spain will have completed all that it is incumbent upon her to do in order to

hasten the end of Cuba's misfortunes. The rest of the
task, *i. e.*, the material and practical application of the
reforms, will not depend for its performance exclusively
upon the mother country in the future. It will also be
necessary that the insurgents, convinced as they must be
of the futility of their struggle, and moved to compassion
by the desolation and ruin of their native land, lay down
their arms soon and allow free play to the inexhaustible
generosity of the mother country, ever ready to take them
back into her fold. Although such hopes may be cherished
as to many of them, perhaps it would be presumptuous to
entertain them as to all. For reasons already set forth
by Your Majesty's Government, it may be deemed probable that there will not be wanting men who, blind to
their own as well as to their country's best interests, will
endeavor to prolong, for however brief a period, the de-
plorable evils which now afflict the Island, imagining, per-
chance, that Spain will tire of her sacrifices and raise the
flag of peace upon any terms, leaving that beautiful land,
together with the lives and property of its loyal inhabitants
enlisted in our cause, at the mercy of the irreconcilable
advocates of separation from the mother country. As to
the present Government, it may here be said that no one
will ever obtain its co-operation in such a course.

But it is time, Your Majesty, to acknowledge that measures of such scope as those herein proposed are not of the
kind that in free countries usually come within the
attributes of the Executive. Only the manifestly extraordinary nature of the present circumstances could have
persuaded Your Majesty's Government to adopt them in
the form of a Decree, upon which the Council of State is
to be heard, and which is to be duly laid before the
Cortes, in order that it may receive from them the utmost
legality that it may require. For less obvious reasons
other governments have considered themselves compelled
to act in like manner, asking afterward for what, bor-

rowing the term from the English, is now called in Spain a " Bill of Indemnity." To have made such a matter the subject of a prolonged and critical discussion while the war is waging would have invited troubles so self-evident that it is needless to particularize them here. Our Constitution itself recognizes in the Crown the right, in the event of a foreign war, both of declaring it and of making and ratifying peace, submitting afterward to the Cortes a documentary report thereon. And although the insurrection in Cuba is not in truth a foreign war, it may well be compared with those of that nature that we have sustained in the past, on account of the vast sacrifices in men and money that it entails upon the nation There are not lacking, therefore, plausible reasons for proceeding in the same manner that the Constitution provides in the case of a war with an independent state. But the Government is not seeking at all to shirk its responsibility in endeavoring by means of this Decree to facilitate the ultimate accomplishment of peace. As the Cabinet is ready to face its responsibility before the Cortes, the respect in which the latter are held by the former simply induces it to present here excuses the validity of which it is incumbent exclusively on them to decide. In the meantime, as the thirteenth paragraph, Section 45, of the organic law of the Council of State requires that this body be consulted in regard to "any innovation in the laws, ordinances, rules and regulations applicable to our trans-oceanic provinces," the present Ministry shall not fail to meet this essential requirement in a matter of such moment as the one under consideration, even if it be only in order to strengthen its own judgment with that of the supreme consultative body of the Realm.

Not all the problems involved in the government of the West Indies will be solved, however, by means of the Decree herewith submitted. Some of them give us time to seek their solution from the Cortes—a course, moreover, which their exceptional character demands. One of these is in reference to the determination, in a precise and absolute manner, of the expenses necessary to the maintenance of sovereignty, and of all other expenses, aside from those purely local, that shall correspond to Cuba, as fixed charges upon her Budget. This is a matter that must be submitted to the Cortes, as it affects the Peninsular provinces equally with those of the Island.

Another of the problems referred to above is the one relative to the judicial organization; for, though all judicial functionaries are already included in one civil list with those of the Peninsula, and though some rules are laid down in the present Decree for their appointment to fill vacancies that correspond to the "turn of selection"* for the West Indies, there remain some essential points to be covered by legislative enactment, among others the proportionate share that the West Indies and the other Spanish provinces shall have in the number of aspirants to the national magistracy.

No reference is made, either, in the present Decree to electoral reform, because certain reasons of a high order bar the introduction by the Government of changes in the existing system for the election of Representatives and Senators, without the concurrence of the Cortes; and

---

* In almost every branch of the Spanish Government service the officers and functionaries thereof are registered in the respective civil list according to rank and to seniority in each rank; and in filling vacancies in any but the lowest rank, the appointing officer is not only obliged to promote one of those registered in the rank immediately inferior to the one in which the vacancy is to be filled, but he is obliged to follow two alternate "turns," viz., to the first vacancy occurring in any given class he is to promote the employee, officer or functionary heading, as senior, the list of the class next inferior in rank, this being termed the "turn of seniority." To the next vacancy occurring in the same class he may promote, at his discretion, any employee, officer or functionary included in the list of the class next inferior in rank, provided that the person so selected is otherwise legally entitled to promotion, there being certain requirements such as a certain number of years of service in each rank. This is called the "turn of discretionary selection."—(*Translator's Note.*)

because to the above system, which is the primary one, all others relative to Provincial Assemblies and Municipalities have always been subordinate.

The Government is not yet in a position to determine how brief or how long the period may be within which the present reforms can be put into effect in Cuba and, consequently, in Porto Rico, although from all the data at hand at the moment of draughting the following Decree the outlook seems very satisfactory and there are many indications that peace is not far off; but, at any rate, the Government feels that it must be prepared to put such reforms into practical operation without delay as soon as may be possible. To this end, therefore, the Council of State shall be immediately consulted, although the Decree of Reforms shall not be enforced until all necessary conditions are complied with. This done, and the intentions of Spain being from this moment known, it is to be hoped that a conciliatory spirit will prevail in the West Indies, thus hastening by easy means that which the country has always longed for; that which the civilized world desires, and that which Your Majesty and the Government, as much or more than anyone else, have striven for in the past and will continue in the future to strive for—a fruitful and lasting peace.

Your Majesty:

I have the honor to be Your Majesty's
Most humble servant,
ANTONIO CANOVAS DEL CASTILLO.

ROYAL DECREE.

Upon the proposition of my Prime Minister, and with the concurrence of the Council of Ministers, in the name of my august son, King Alfonso XIII., and as Queen Regent of the Kingdom, I hereby decree, as follows:

Sole Section.—The plan for extending the scope of the reforms for the Island of Cuba which were embodied in the law of March 15, 1895, and which plan shall in due time apply as well to the reforms already put in force in Porto Rico, shall be submitted to the full Council of State, for its prompt consideration and report, in accordance with the provisions of Section 45, paragraph 13, of the organic law of that Supreme National Advisory Body.

Given in the Palace on the fourth day of February, in the year one thousand eight hundred and ninety-seven.

MARIA CRISTINA.

The Prime Minister,
ANTONIO CANOVAS DEL CASTILLO.

PLAN FOR THE EXTENSION IN SCOPE

REFORM LAW OF MARCH 15, 1895.

———•◆•———

Article 1.

The Law of March 15, 1895, relative to Reforms in the system of Government and Civil Administration in the Island of Cuba, shall be extended and given a wider scope in accordance with the following bases, which so far as may be necessary shall be amplified and developed by means of Rules and Regulations.

Basis I.—The Boards of Aldermen and the Provincial Assemblies of the Island of Cuba shall enjoy such liberty of action as may be compatible with observance of law and with the rights of private individuals.

Powers of the Provincial Assemblies and Boards of Aldermen.

They shall be free to appoint and remove all their employees.

The Presidents of the Provincial Assemblies shall be elected by said assemblies from among their own members. In each Provincial Assembly there shall be a Provincial Executive Committee, consisting of Assemblymen elected semi-annually by the Assembly. The Provincial Executive Committee shall elect its chairman.

Mayors and Deputy Mayors shall be elected to the respective offices by the Board of Aldermen from among their own members. The Mayors shall without limitation exercise the executive functions of the municipal government, as the executive officers of the Boards of Aldermen.

Mayors: How Elected.

A Provincial Assembly may stay the execution of resolutions adopted by any of the Boards of Aldermen under its jurisdiction; it may also censure, warn, fine or suspend the members thereof, whenever said members shall exceed the limits of their municipal jurisdiction; in such case the Assembly shall report such action to the Civil Governor for his approval and for its execution.

Should the Civil Governor not approve the action of the Provincial Assembly, either in whole or in part, said Assembly may appeal to the full Supreme Court of the corresponding territory, whose decision shall be final.

The Raising of Revenue. For the purpose of raising the revenue necessary to meet their expenses and obligations, the Municipal Councils and Provincial Assemblies shall be vested with all the authority compatible with the system of taxation governing the general and local Budgets of the Island; it being understood that the revenues for the provincial Budgets shall be independent of those for the municipal Budgets.

Public Education. The establishment of public educational institutions in the provinces shall devolve exclusively upon their respective Provincial Assemblies, and of those in the cities and towns upon the Boards of Aldermen.

The Governor General and the Civil Governors shall have the right of intervention in these matters only to the extent necessary to insure compliance with the general laws, and to satisfy themselves that the new charges imposed by the local Budgets are not in excess of the respective provincial and municipal resources.

Financial Statements by the Mayors. The annual financial statements rendered by the Mayors, which shall include all receipts and expenditures, both ordinary and special, shall be published in their respective localities, and whatever may be their total amount shall be audited, and objected to or approved, as the case may be, by the Municipal Council, after hearing any protests offered against them. From the action of the Municipal Council appeal may be taken to the Provincial Executive Committee, and in cases where the latter shall declare the liability of any official or officials, an appeal may be taken to the full Supreme Court of each respective district, which shall decide, without further recourse, in conformity with the administrative and penal laws that may be applicable thereto.

Basis II.—The Council of Administration shall consist of thirty-five Councilors. Of these, twenty-one shall be elected as follows by the same voters who are entitled to suffrage at the elections for Assemblymen and Aldermen, and according to the provisions of Article III. of the Reform law of March 15, 1895, as follows: Five by the Province of Havana, four each by the Provinces of Santa Clara and Santiago de Cuba, three each by the Provinces of Pinar del Rio and Matanzas, and two by the Province of Puerto Principe. Nine other Councilors shall be the following: The Rector of the University of Havana, the President of the Havana Chamber of Commerce, the President of the Economical Society of the Friends of the Country, the President of the Sugar Planters' Association, the President of the Tobacco Manufacturers' Union, a member of the Chapters of the Cathedrals of Havana and Santiago de Cuba, which Chapters, assembled as electoral colleges, shall elect such member every four years; a representative of all the trades associations of Havana, to be chosen every fourth year by the presidents of such trade associations, and two Councilors representing the principal taxpayers of the Province of Havana, to be elected every four years, one by the hundred citizens paying the highest taxes on real estate and the other by the hundred paying the highest taxes on industries, commerce, arts and professions. The remaining five Councilors shall be the Senators or Representatives to the Cortes who shall have been elected the greatest number of times at general elections, seniority of age determining where other conditions are equal.

The Governor General shall be the *Honorary* President of the Council, and he shall preside, without vote, at any session he may attend. The regular President shall be

Council of Administration: How Constituted.

President of the Council.

— 17 —

appointed by the Governor General from among its members.

The office of Councilor shall be without compensation, shall carry personal liability, and, once accepted, cannot be resigned except for cause. The office shall also be incompatible with that of Representative to the Cortes or Senator, and anyone eligible to the two shall elect between them within two months.

Candidates having the qualifications necessary for election as Representatives to the Cortes, and having resided two years on the Island, may be elected Councilors.

In no case shall those debarred from election as Representatives to the Cortes by Section 19 of the Provincial Law, now in force, be elected Councilors.

The Council shall have a Secretary's office, with an adequate force for the transaction of the affairs hereby assigned to it.

Appointment and Removal of the Council's Employees. The power of appointment and removal of all employees of the Secretary's office shall be solely and exclusively vested in the Council.

The Council shall elect every six months a Committee on Reports, whose duty shall be to report upon all matters coming within the jurisdiction of the Council.

Said committee shall consist of five Councilors, each of whom shall be entitled to such compensation as the Council may determine, but which shall not exceed the sum of $2,000 for each term of six months.

Expenses Inherent to Sovereignty. *Basis III.*—The Cortes shall determine the expenditures, which shall necessarily be chargeable as expenses inherent to sovereignty, and every three years shall fix the total amount of revenue required therefor; this without prejudice to the right of the Cortes to alter this provision.

Levying of Taxes. The Council of Administration shall each year levy such taxes and imposts as may be necessary to provide the total amount of revenue required and to meet the expenditures approved by the Cortes in the national Budget for the Island; this without prejudice to the constitutional right of the Cortes to introduce such changes as it may deem proper in the premises.

The Council of Administration may renounce the powers conferred upon it by the last preceding paragraph; in which case it shall be understood that it also renounces, for the term covered by the Budget, the powers conferred by Sections 1 and 2 of the first paragraph, Basis IV.

Should the Council of Administration surrender said powers, or should it fail on the first day of June of any year to levy the taxes and imposts for the revenue required to meet the expenditures included in the national Budget for the Island, the Governor General shall supply such default, so far as it may exist, and either in part or in whole, through the Chief of the Treasury.

The Council of Administration shall also prepare and approve every year the local Budget for the Island of Cuba, in order to make provision for such branches of the public service as are intrusted to it. It shall also include in said Budget the necessary appropriations for the personnel and the supplies for the office of the Secretary of the General Government of Cuba, for the Bureau of Local Administration, for the Department of Finance, for the office of the Auditor, and for the offices of the six Provincial Governors of the Island, which expenses are hereby declared to be obligatory charges upon said Budget. **The Council to Prepare Budgets.**

In regard to the obligatory charges just mentioned, the Governor General shall, should the case arise, become vested with the powers mentioned in the fourth paragraph of the present basis, relative to the national Budget for the Island.

Should any changes or modifications adopted by the Council of Administration affecting services chargeable, as fixed obligations, against the local Budget for the Island, not be approved by the Governor General, they shall be submitted to the Minister for the Colonies for final action, to be taken by resolution of the Cabinet, after first obtaining a report thereon from the Council of State. In default of any action by the Minister within two months, the action of the Council of Administration shall stand.

The Council of Administration shall approve the local Budget for the Island before the first day of June in each year.

Revenues for Local Budgets. The revenues of the local Budget, besides those already provided, shall consist of such taxes and imposts as the Council of Administration may determine and as shall not conflict with the sources of revenue applied to the national Budget for the Island.

Educational Institutions. The establishment of new educational institutions preparatory for the various Government services*, the Army and Navy excepted, shall devolve upon the Council of Administration, whenever such institutions shall be of a general character and for the benefit of the entire Island.

The Council of Administration may file with the Governor General claims or protests, should there be occasion for them, against any resolution or action taken by the Chief of the Bureau of Local Administration.

Powers of the Council in the Matter of Customs Tariff. *Basis IV.*—The Council of Administration shall have the following powers in the matter of customs tariff:

1. To make, upon the recommendation of the Chief of the Treasury of the Island, the rules and regulations for the administration of the customs revenue.

2. To take such action as it may deem advisable, with the advice of the Chief of the Treasury, or upon his recommendation, in regard to export duties.

3. To fix or change at its discretion, with the advice of the Chief of the Treasury, or upon his recommendation,

* See notes on pages 10 and 25.

the fiscal duties to be levied upon imports through the Custom Houses of the Island of Cuba.

4. To report upon and to recommend any changes which experience may suggest in the general or supplementary dispositions of the tariff, or in the schedules, notes or repertory thereof; said report to necessarily precede any action taken thereon.

These powers are granted subject to the following limitations :

1. A reasonable and necessary protection shall be maintained in favor of national products and manufactures, provided they be directly of national origin, as regards their importation into the Island of Cuba; such protection to be accorded by means of differential duties to be levied at the minimum rates, hereafter to be determined, equally upon all products of foreign origin. **Protection to National Products.**

2. The fiscal duties to be fixed by the Council of Administration shall not be differential, but must apply equally upon all imports, those of national origin included.

3. Such export duties as may be established shall not be differential, but shall be applied equally to the same class of products, whatever their destination. Exception may be made, however, in favor of products exported directly for national consumption, in which exclusive case the Council of Administration may grant exemption from or a differential reduction in the duties by it established. **Export Duties.**

4. The prohibition to export any product, should this at any time be ordered, shall not apply to products exported directly for national consumption.

5. The powers granted by virtue of Sections 1 and 2 of the first paragraph of this present basis shall be exercised by the Council of Administration or, in default thereof, by the Governor General, in accordance with the obligations imposed by the second paragraph, Basis III. The fiscal import duties, and also the export duties, should such be established, shall remain unchanged during the term cov-

ered by the Budget which is based upon the revenues that those duties are estimated to provide.

The import tariff shall be embodied in the following form : The duties shall be set forth in two columns, viz., the first shall contain the fiscal duties to be levied and collected on all importations of whatever origin, national included ; the second shall contain the differential duties to be levied equally upon all products of foreign origin; these last mentioned duties to constitute the necessary protection which is secured to national products and manufactures.

The fiscal duties comprised in the first or general column may be freely altered by the addition of such extra rates of duties and by such reductions or exemptions as the Council of Administration may determine, in the exercise of the powers hereinbefore granted, subject to the limitations also hereinbefore expressed.

The Cortes shall determine the maximum of protection to be maintained in favor of national products and manufactures. The maximum thus established shall not be altered without the concurrence of the Cortes, and this concurrence shall also be necessary for any changes in the column of differential duties.

The initial duties to be levied upon all the articles comprised in the various schedules of the tariff and which are to constitute, for the first time, the differential column before mentioned, shall be fixed by the Government.

These differential duties, which need not in general be higher than 20 per cent. *ad valorem*, shall not exceed 35 per cent. *ad valorem*, even on such articles as may require this exceptional and maximum rate. A special act of the Cortes shall be required in order to exceed the above limit of 35 per cent. on any article. Such act may raise the limit to 40 per cent. *ad valorem*.

The Government shall order a revision of the official schedules of valuations of merchandise after a full hearing of all interests. Whenever, as a result of the revision of said **Revision of Schedules of Valuation.** schedule of valuations, and by reason of the limitations established by the preceding rule, it shall appear that a reduction should be made in the differential duty on any specified article of the Tariff, the finding of said fact shall of itself operate to effect such reduction. The official schedules of valuation of merchandise, once revised, shall remain unchanged for the term of ten years, unless otherwise provided by the Cortes.

It being impossible to carry immediately into effect all **Provisional Tariff.** the provisions that this basis establishes for the future, and it being deemed inadvisable to further delay the revision of the Tariff now in operation in Cuba, the Minister for the Colonies shall, by virtue of legal authority now vested in him, and in accordance with the law of June 28, 1895, publish and put into effect a provisional Tariff, the general lines and the schedules of which shall be adjusted to the requirements of this present basis; and the fiscal duties which may be thus fixed and which may appear in their respective column, and also whatever may relate to export duties or regulations, shall be provisionally put into force.

Commercial treaties or conventions which shall affect **Commercial Treaties.** the customs tariff of the Island of Cuba must be of a special character. The benefits of the clause of the " most favored nation," or any equivalent thereof, shall not be granted therein. The Council of Administration shall be consulted as to the advisability of granting any special concessions which the Government may have in view, in negotiating any treaty, before the latter shall be completed for submission to the Cortes.

Basis V.—The Governor General shall have the power **Power of Appointment of Employees.** to appoint and remove all the employees of the office of the Secretary of the General Government of the Island, of the Bureau of Civil and Economic Administration and of the Provincial Governments, as provided in Basis VII.

Basis VI.—The office of the Secretary of the General Government shall be under the direction of a Superior Chief of Administration.

Chiefs of Bureaus to Nominate Appointees. The Chief of the Treasury of the Island of Cuba, the Comptroller and the Chief of the Bureau of Local Administration shall propose to the Governor General the appointment of all the employees of their respective offices, according to the provisions of Basis VII., and they may likewise propose their removal.

Postal and Telegraph Service. The Bureau of Posts and Telegraphs, under the direction of a Chief of Administration, shall have under its charge the services relative to postal and telegraphic communications, both land and maritime, for which the Council of Administration may make provision; and it shall be its duty to examine and render annually the accounts of said services and to execute all the resolutions of the Council concerning the Bureau.

Employees to Be Natives or Residents of Cuba. **Basis VII.**—All the employees of the Civil and Economic Administration of the Island of Cuba, with the exception of the Secretary of the General Government, the Chief of the Treasury, the Comptroller, the Chiefs of the Bureaus of Local Administration and of Posts and Telegraphs, and the Civil Governors of the six Provinces, shall be appointed, as vacancies occur, by the Governor General of the Island of Cuba, in conformity with existing laws or with such as may be hereafter enacted, from among the natives of said Island or from among others residing or having resided there during two consecutive years.

The Governor General shall submit to the Council of Administration, for its cognizance, evidence of the legal qualifications of all appointees.

In the appointment of all functionaries belonging to the

civil service professions* and to the postal and telegraph Civil Service Provisions.
service, the legal dispositions and rules and regulations relating thereto shall be complied with.

The employees of the office of the Secretary of the General Government and of the offices of the Provincial Governors shall be appointed and removed by the Governor General at his discretion. The employees of the Bureau of Local Administration, of the Treasury and of the Administration of Customs (except in case a corps of experts be organized) and of the office of the Comptroller, shall be appointed by the Governor General upon the nomination of the respective chiefs of the above mentioned branches of the service. They may be removed by the Governor General upon the proposition of said chiefs, or directly by the former whenever he shall deem it necessary.

The Governor General may appoint Supervisors of Supervisors of Public Education. Public Education; two each for the Provinces of Havana, Santa Clara and Santiago de Cuba, and one each for the Provinces of Pinar del Rio, Matanzas and Puerto Principe.

The Governor General may also appoint, upon the nomi- Deputies to Represent Civil Governors in Towns. nation of the Provincial Governors, Deputies representing the latter authorities in the municipal districts. Said Deputies shall have gubernatorial authority in their respective localities and shall have control of the police

---

* Various branches of the Government service in Spain constitute what are termed state or civil service professions. Admission thereto can only be obtained through a special course of studies for each, and after a rigid competitive examination for such vacancies in the lowest rank as from time to time are to be filled. Once admitted, members of said professions cannot be removed from office, except after trial for cause, though they may be assigned to different posts pertaining to their respective ranks; and their advancement is regulated by a system which, while securing to all equal justice in promotion by seniority, still offers to all an incentive to zeal and efficiency. See note on foot of page 10. At a certain age, and after a given number of years' service, members of civil service professions may retire with a pension, proportionate to their rank on retirement.—*Translator's Note.*

force. In no case shall they interfere with the Mayors or Boards of Aldermen in the exercise of their powers.

The Governor General, whenever he shall deem it advisable, and acting upon the recommendation of the Provincial Governors, may in the same manner deputize the Mayor of any city or town.

Administration of Justice.

Basis VIII.—Any vacancies which may hereafter occur in any of the offices under the Administration of Justice* and the appointment to which may, according to turn, be discretionary,** shall be filled by the Minister for the Colonies, either from natives of the Island of Cuba or from those who reside or may have resided there. Applications for appointment, accompanied by the records of the respective applicants, shall be filed with the Presidents of the Supreme Courts of the various districts, and shall be forwarded to the Department through the Governor General.

Municipal Judges.

The Municipal Judge of each judicial district shall be appointed by the Governor General, who shall select for that office one of three persons to be nominated by the Aldermen of the respective municipalities and by the voters entitled to vote for the electors of Senators, regard being had to the provisions of the law relative to the appointment of electors.

In municipalities where two or more Judges are to be appointed separate ballots shall becast for each set of nominees in the manner above provided.

The Municipal Judges who may be elected must possess the qualifications prescribed by the existing laws in the Island of Cuba.

Council to Respect Pending Contracts.

Basis IX.—The Council of Administration shall respect pending contracts throughout the various branches of the

---

* This comprises Judges and Prosecuting Attorneys.— *T. N.*
** See note foot of page 25.

Government service and of the Treasury of the Island, and upon their expiration may renew them or not at its discretion.

The Council of Administration is hereby empowered to apply to the Island of Cuba the Law regulating the operations of the Treasury which is now in force in the Peninsula, and to enter into an agreement for that purpose with the Spanish Bank of the Island of Cuba.

Council Empowered to Contract for Collection of Taxes.

The Council is further empowered to intrust the above mentioned Bank with the collection of revenues, or to contract with it with reference thereto, subject always to the approval of the Minister for the Colonies.

Basis X.—A special Decree, which shall be reported to the Cortes, shall contain such dispositions as may be deemed necessary for the preservation of the public peace and for the suppression of any separatist movement which by any means whatever may be again set on foot.

Preservation of the Public Peace.

Article 2.

The Government shall embody in a single instrument the foregoing provisions and the provisions of the reform law of March 15, 1895, so as to harmonize the two; and shall in due time report the same to the Cortes.

Previous and Present Reform Measures to Be Adjusted.

These united provisions shall be supplemented by rules and regulations to be subsequently formulated, which, however, shall in no manner change the intent or meaning thereof, and whose sole purpose shall be to adjust the said provisions to other legislation now in force, as provided in the before mentioned law of March 15, 1895.

Upon the issuing of an order putting into effect in Cuba the provisions of the law of March 15, 1895, and the provisions of this Royal Decree, said provisions shall, so far

These Dispositions to Have the Force of Law.

as may be possible, have all the force of law, without prejudice to the rules and regulations subsequently to be made.

Article 3.

Reforms Applied to Porto Rico.

The provisions of the present Decree, as an extension in scope of the law of March 15, 1895, shall be applied to the Island of Porto Rico wherever compatible with the different conditions prevailing in said Island and with the institutions already established there.

The rules and regulations already issued for Porto Rico shall be amended so far as may be necessary to bring them into accord with those which shall be issued for the Island of Cuba.

Article 4.

When the Reforms Shall Be Put Into Effect.

The date upon which the provisions of the reform law of March 15, 1895, shall be put into effect in Cuba, and upon which the provisions of this supplementary Decree shall be applied to both Cuba and Porto Rico, shall be determined by the Government as soon as the condition of the war in Cuba shall permit.

The Prime Minister,

ANTONIO CANOVAS DEL CASTILLO.

MADRID, February 4, 1897.

. COMMENTARY.

Points to Be Borne in Mind in Reading the Foregoing Decree.

IN perusing the official text of the " Expository Preamble " and " Royal Decree " embodying the reform measures recently adopted by Spain for the government of the Island of Cuba, which is herein rendered in as faithful an English version as the difference in construction of the two languages would permit of, the reader will undoubtedly have a better comprehension of those measures and a more adequate appreciation of their scope if he will bear in mind: First—The political complexion of the party whose leader, as Premier of the Kingdom, has prepared and obtained the sanction of the Crown for such a radical measure of Spanish colonial policy. Second—The purpose which has actuated Her Majesty's Government in adopting such a course, and its intentions as to the development and application of the plan of reforms. Third—The view taken in regard to this plan by the leaders of other Spanish political parties. Fourth—The spirit in which its announcement has been received in Cuba by prominent natives and influential Peninsular-born residents. Fifth—The trend of public opinion in foreign countries on the reforms.

As an aid, therefore, to those not thoroughly acquainted with the subject, the writer here presents, supplemented by a few remarks of his own, various statements and expressions of opinion covering the points above enumerated, which he has culled, extracted and rendered into English, where necessary, from such matter as he has at hand.

As to the first point, it is well to remember that while the Conservative party, under the leadership of the present

Prime Minister, Señor Canovas del Castillo, has always, true to its name and creed, opposed radical legislation and the adoption of political measures for which it did not consider the time ripe nor the people of Spain prepared, it has almost invariably, when called into power, respected or "conserved" all successive political rights enacted into the Laws of the Realm through the initiative of the Liberal party. And in many instances, as in the present Cuban question, the Conservatives have forestalled the more advanced party in the granting of reforms, going even beyond the limits predetermined by the latter's declarations of principles as to certain issues.

Conservative Party Forestalls the Liberals in Granting Reforms.

Thus, not only did the Conservative party, then in the opposition, heartily support and solidly vote in favor of the Abarzuza Cuban Reform bill, draughted and submitted to the Cortes by the Liberal Cabinet of Premier Sagasta in 1895, but now, while under the tremendous responsibilities inherent to power in such critical circumstances as Spain is going through, Señor Canovas boldly steps far beyond the boundaries pointed out by the promises of other Spanish statesmen or even by the demands of the several Cuban legal political parties, the Autonomist party alone excepted.

Intentions of the Government.

In regard to the second point, Señor Canovas del Castillo made the following statement on the day in which the Royal Decree was published in the *Gaceta de Madrid* (official organ of record). These utterances of the eminent Spanish statesman confirm and throw additional light on that noble and remarkable official writing : the " Expository Preamble" to the Royal Decree.

To a press representative Señor Canovas said :

I have devoted much study and thought to the preparation of the plan of reforms, and being inspired by the utmost sincerity I have endeavored to imbue the measure with the broadest spirit.

It has been my aim to make of the reforms a national undertaking; I have worked on them, therefore, on behalf of my country and for my country.

My idea, my determination, is to put them into effect according to the most liberal interpretation and with absolute sincerity.

Sr. Canovas del Castillo's Statement.

With entire good faith I am resolutely going toward the establishment of autonomy in Cuba. On this line no radicalism can check me. What I have been most careful of is not to leave any loophole for independence. And in this I have fulfilled my duty.

*　　　*　　　*　　　*　　　*　　　*

It is not necessary to await the complete pacification of the Island of Cuba in order to put the reforms into practical operation.

Application of the Plan of Reforms.

As soon the rebellion is reduced to the Oriental Department all the pacified provinces shall immediately enter upon the enjoyment of the advantages to be derived from the new measures. Without further delay the Boards of Aldermen and the Provincial Assemblies shall be elected in those provinces, and they shall have entire liberty of action without any Government intervention. And thus the entire plan of reforms shall be rapidly developed, with a view of having it in practical operation in as short a period as possible.

In connection with this same point, i. e., the intentions of the Spanish Government as to the development and application of its plan of reforms, it will be proper to transcribe here the statements made by the Spanish Minister in Washington, Señor Dupuy de Lôme, to a representative of The United Associated Presses on the 7th of last February.

Sr. Dupuy de Lôme's Statement.

A close study of the course of the Cuban question could not but convey to the least observing mind the conviction that this most efficient and able diplomat enjoys to more than an ordinary degree the confidence of his Government. It is but fair to assume, therefore, especially if it be remembered how discreet and cautious have been all Señor Dupuy de Lôme's utterances, that in the following statement the Spanish representative reflects the purpose of his Government; or, in other words, that he gives, *unofficially*, expression to certain knowledge, *officially acquired*, bearing on the question under review.

His statement, in substance, as published is as follows:

Electoral Reforms. The electoral reforms were not referred to at length in the decree of the Ministry, for the reasons stated in the preamble of Señor Canovas, that they will require the action of the Cortes. I am informed, however, that the Government will not oppose the extension of the basis of the suffrage, but they desire to do it in such a way as to prevent undue influence being acquired by the illiterate portion of the population.

The present law requires the payment of taxes amounting in the aggregate to $5, except where the privilege of voting is extended to the graduates of the universities and other members of the learned professions. Any educational qualification which may be suggested by the Cubans, and which seems reasonable and proper, will undoubtedly be adopted by the Cortes. The subject must be regulated by that body.

It is the purpose of the Government to show the greatest generosity toward the insurgents who lay down their arms. The reforms cannot well be put into full effect until the sovereignty of Spain is acknowledged. The Government will not relax its military activity in any degree if the insurgents show a disposition to continue the contest and fail to appreciate the great concessions made by the home Government.

Spain's Generous Spirit in Dealing with Cuba. Spain has gone to the utmost limit in her generosity to the Cuban people, and has established a system by which the Island will hereafter be governed in Cuba by residents of the Island, instead of being governed from Madrid. The right to hold office is given to Spaniards who have lived two years in Cuba, because they have become in a large degree identified with the interests of the Island.

In this respect the proposed policy is not unlike that which has been pursued by the United States, where members of both political parties have delighted to honor citizens born outside of the country. Conspicuous examples are found in the cases of Mr. Wilson, of Iowa, who is to be a member of the Cabinet of your next President, and who was, I believe, born in Scotland, and of Carl Schurz, who was born in Germany, but was Secretary of the Interior under the administration of President Hayes.

The tariff features of the new Decree are very comprehensive in their scope, and mean a great deal for the United States as well as for Cuba. The duties levied will be equal against all countries except Spain; and American manufacturers and exporters, in view of their familiarity with Cuban trade and their nearness to the Island, are likely to appreciate the importance of these concessions.

The situation will be much more favorable to American trade than under the reciprocity treaty of 1890. There were in that treaty two schedules for American goods, one of 25 per cent. and another of 50 per cent., but Spain had the right to provide for the entry of her products free of duty, thus giving her a marked advantage over the United States. The Spanish West Indies are the best consumers of United States products that you have on this continent. It will be necessary for the home Government to consult the Cubans before a reciprocity treaty is concluded. The new reforms distinctly provide that such treaties may be suggested by the new Council of Administration.

The Council of Administration shall not only contain twenty-one members elected by the qualified voters of Cuba, but will contain Cubans among the other members, if they possess the qualifications to attain the position which entitles them to seats. The members of the Council of Administration, who shall sit by virtue of their office as Presidents of the Chamber of Commerce, the Planters' Association and other bodies, may just as well be Cubans as persons born in Spain, if they show the qualities which naturally advance them to those places. The places are entirely open to native Cubans as well as Spaniards.

The Liberal party, upon returning to power, could or would never attempt to take a step backward on such a vital national issue, either by reactionary legislation or by a narrow interpretation of the measures enacted by the Conservatives.

That is not only self-evident, but it is assured beyond peradventure by the fact that the leaders of the Liberal party have approved of the new plan of reforms. In effect, Señor Maura, who in colonial matters can speak with best authority on behalf of said party, he being the author of the Reform bill of 1893, has said:

The Royal Decree issued by the Prime Minister unfolds with vigorous frankness a system which differs much more

The Tariff
Features.

More Favorable to the United States than the Reciprocity Treaty.

The Liberal Party Indorses the Plan of Reforms.

radically from that now established in the West Indies than did the Law of 1895* or the Bill of 1893.** It adopts principles and lays down bases which should satisfy all aspirations, that are not insatiable, of the liberal political parties in Cuba. I spurn as absurd any insinuation to the effect that the scope of the reforms may be impaired by the rules and regulations and other means for their application, because no statesman should be insulted by imputing such bad faith to him, nor would any fail to perceive the dangers of so acting.

The Republicans Also. The present reform measures also meet the favor of the Spanish Republicans, as is evidenced by the following words from their leader, the great orator, Don Emilio Castelar:

I, as a writer, can only applaud the tendencies of the reform decrees. I approve them with all my heart, and support them with all my power. I oppose any design of reducing them, whatever be its origin.

With the projects of Maura, Abarzuza and Canovas, all defended by me, we have dealt justice to Cuba, establishing her self-government and developing her commercial relations.

From them good, nothing but good, can come. Therefore I am satisfied, and thus you have my opinion.

As to how the reforms will be accepted by the political parties in Cuba, by influential organizations of the Island and by Cuban public opinion in general, the following excerpts from statements thereon may give a fair idea. **The Cuban Autonomists Approve of the Reform Measures.** Those from the leaders of the Autonomist party, who are also Members of the Cortes, are of the utmost importance, because the principles and ideals of this party undoubtedly represent the aspirations of the majority of native residents of the Island, and because it is more than likely

---

* In force in Porto Rico, but not yet applied to Cuba on account of the insurrection.

** Of which Señor Maura, then Minister for the Colonies, was author, but which did not become law on account of his leaving the portfolio.

that to its banners shall rally the better class of those who have participated in the present insurrection, as soon as the latter is finally put down.

Here are the extracts above referred to:

From Señor Rafael Móntoro, a native of Cuba, one of the leaders of the Autonomist party and Member of the Cortes for the Island: Statement of Sr. Montoro.

It is difficult to make quite clear to the Anglo-Saxon mind what will be the political relations in Cuba to the mother country in the new era which is dawning. It is impossible to reason by analogy and contrast with the British colonies, because, to cite merely one cause of essential difference, Spain has a written Constitution which is the palladium and supreme guarantee of our liberties, and Great Britain is ruled by a more flexible and an unwritten Constitution. A New Era Is Dawning.

Our Constitution establishes a certain identity of civil and political rights between all subjects of the Crown, and it provides that we Cubans must have our representatives in the Cortes, as do all other provinces of the kingdom.

Our suffrage for the election of Deputies to the Cortes is even now, in my opinion, sufficiently ample, but it will be even more extensive under the new régime, so that the voice of Cuba may be heard on all questions of finance and of foreign affairs which interest and affect alike all portions of the kingdom. Suffrage in Cuba Is Sufficiently, Ample.

In connection and in harmony with the Local Assembly of Cuba there is no room for doubting that the national or imperial Cortes will grant to us the fullest powers of self-administration and self-government that are possible under our Constitution and compatible with the unity of the Kingdom.

I think that the Spanish Government will have fully satisfied every reasonable and practical demand of the Cuban people. I expect that then the respectable but misguided elements of the insurrection will withdraw from the field, and that there will remain under arms only lawless adventurers and irreconcilable enemies of law and order. The Reasonable Demands of the Cubans Fully Satisfied.

The question of the adjustment of the indebtedness ensuing out of the war is, I admit, a difficult one, perhaps the most difficult one which the situation presents, but it is not an insuperable obstacle to peace, as some especially ill-informed publicists in foreign countries represent it to be. Adjustment of the War Debt Not an Insurmountable Obstacle.

I believe the subject can be reasonably and equitably set-

— 35 —

tled by an arrangement between the Spanish and Cuban treasuries.

Also from Señor Montoro, on another occasion, conjointly with Señor José A. del Cueto, likewise a prominent member of the Autonomist party:

In our opinion the reform measure is of the utmost importance, since the institutions based thereon are remarkably liberal, and the changes introduced in the present system are very radical. If understood and loyally appreciated they reveal the noble fulfillment of the promises contained in the Crown Speech and explained in the memorable summing up of the debate in the Cortes on the 15th of July last by Señor Canovas.

The New Measure Contains All Essential Elements of Self=Government.

We believe that the above measure contains all the essential elements of self-government, and that the amendments and extensions in scope that it may require in order to reach all the development possible within the national Constitution may well be left to the action of time, of public opinion and of local initiative, when, peace being restored, it will become possible for them to manifest themselves authoritatively. The Expository Preamble of the Royal Decree opens reasonable horizons to every loyal aspiration in that direction.

The effects of the reform measure upon the public spirit cannot but be very favorable at the present moment, and they shall be more so according as the intentions of the Government become known.

Sr. Labra's Statement.

From Señor Labra, a distinguished Cuban jurist, Autonomist Member of the Cortes for the Island:

Señor Canovas' plan of reforms implies a laudable change in the course of our colonial policy. It is necessary that we work on that basis. We may now expect from the Liberal Peninsular party a new determination and a more decided spirit in its attitude and in its course, since the step in advance taken by the Conservative party is really an exceptional one.

Autonomy the Best Guarantor of the Nation's Integrity.

As for me personally, I may say that I have never been pessimistic in politics, and that I have to-day additional reasons for reaffirming what I have always held, that colonial autonomy is the best guarantor of the honor, the strength and the integrity of the nation.

Sr. Fernando de Castro's Statement.

From Señor Rafael Fernandez de Castro, a Cuban Autonomist, ex-Member of the Cortes for the Island:

The reforms represent a great progressive stride in Spanish colonial policy. They are more liberal than those

— 36 —

embodied in the Reform Law of March 15, 1895, and of course more of a fundamental nature than those prepared in his bill by Mr. Maura in 1893. They are equivalent to a grand and decisive entry into a régime that the wise nature of things has been demanding here for some time; that of Autonomy.

From Señor Arturo Amblar, Member of the Cortes for the Island of Cuba:

I believe that the reforms will completely satisfy the long felt wishes of the people of Cuba, and that although they contain details of secondary importance that in practice will be corrected, they may be the means of bringing together many men hitherto of clashing opinions, and of gaining supporters to the national cause.

From Señor Rabel, leader of the Cuban Reformist party, in a cable dispatch to Premier Canovas :

The executive committee of Reformist party, upon learning of reform measures, has resolved to compliment Your Excellency for the broad spirit that they reveal. By such consistent action Your Excellency will satisfy the legitimate aspirations of the people of this Island, who confidently expect the development of the plan of reforms, with the sincere co-operation of all the loyal elements of Cuba, in order to bring about peace, which everyone desires.
The general applause with which the reform measures have been received is the best evidence of their merit.

From Marquis of Apezteguia, a native of Cuba and leader of the Union Constitucional party (this, being the "Tory" or Conservative party of the Island, has always opposed reform measures for Cuba in the direction of self-government) :

The Union Constitucional party cannot oppose the work of the Government. I have come to the Peninsula for the purpose of avoiding friction and in the interest of harmony. As to the effects of the reforms in Cuba, I believe that they will have none directly upon the insurgents in arms. But the new measures will appeal to the reason of the pacific native elements and to foreigners in general, and this moral force on our side will undoubtedly weaken the direct or indirect support that the insurrection has received in some countries.

Voice of the Havana Chamber of Commerce.

From Señor Rosendo Fernandez, President pro tem. of the Havana Chamber of Commerce:

I am positive that this Chamber of Commerce will nobly aid the Government in every measure tending to the attainment of peace and to the fostering of the moral and material interests of the Island on the indisputable basis of Spain's sovereignty.

The Produce Exchange in Favor of the Reforms.

From Señor Marcelino Gonzales, President of the Havana Produce Exchange:

The reforms having been studied out and prepared by so eminent a statesman as Señor Canovas del Castillo, and embodying, as the press reports show, such liberal measures of self-government, they cannot but be beneficial to commerce in general, which shall have more within reach the means of overcoming the obstacles it may encounter in the development of its foreign trade.

Favorable Opinion of the Importers' League.

From Señor Laureano Rodriguez, President of the Cuban Importers' League:

It is my opinion that the reforms, after a revision of the electoral census (enrolment), when put into operation in a spirit of good faith, will satisfy the aspirations of the inhabitants of this Island.

CUBAN PRESS COMMENTS.

From *El País*, organ of the Autonomist party:

The Cuban
Press.

The reforms should be received with satisfaction and
applause, and they should meet with our sincere co-operation, for they go much further in the direction of self-government than the plans of either Señor Abarzuza or Señor
Maura.

From the *Diario de la Matina*, organ of the Reformist
party:

Thanks to the reforms we can now confidently say that the
misfortunes of the Island of Cuba are soon to end.

From *La Lucha*, Republican organ:

The time has come for every honest man who has the welfare of Cuba at heart to exert all his influence and all his
endeavors toward convincing those who are at present in
arms that there exists no longer the reasons or the pretexts
with which they pretended to justify their rebellion.

From *La Union Constitucional*, organ of the party of
that name (Conservative):

The Union Constitucional party will not set any obstacles in the way of the solutions which the home Government has prepared to the difficulties that beset out common
country.

From *El Diario del Ejercito*, organ of the army:

Señor Canovas has once more shown the deep interest he
takes in Cuban affairs by granting the Island such reforms as
the spirit of the times and the public requirements demanded.

FOREIGN PRESS COMMENTS.

From *Le Gaulois*, of Paris:

As a whole the reforms planned by the Madrid Government are of a nature calculated to satisfy the aspirations of Cubans. If the latter should not consider themselves satisfied they would forfeit the sympathy of European nations, who understand perfectly that the Spanish Government in granting to Cuba such liberal laws has gone in one bound to the limit which its dignity and its duty would allow.

From *L'Eclair*, of Paris:

We must admit that in these circumstances Señor Canovas has not revealed himself a Conservative after the fashion of Guizot, who remained unmoved even while he foresaw progress. Señor Canovas resembles rather the great British Conservative Robert Peel, who in 1846 did not hesitate to split his party in order to grant political liberties to the British people.

From *Le Temps*, of Paris:

If Señor Canovas del Castillo considers it necessary to grant to Cuba ample concessions it is, in the first placed because the urgency of establishing the reforms has appeared perfectly clear to him, and, in the second place, because he is perfectly satisfied that he can put them into effect without prejudice to Spain's honor or Spain's interests.

The dispositions of the foregoing Royal Decree being directed to the modification and extension in scope of the Reform Law of March 15, 1895, a proper understanding of the former requires that the latter be referred to, and for this purpose the text in English of that law is hereunto appended.

REFORM LAW OF MARCH 15, 1895.

LAW FOR THE REORGANIZATION OF THE GOVERNMENT AND CIVIL ADMINISTRATION OF THE ISLAND OF CUBA.

Alfonso XIII., by the Grace of God and the Constitution, King of Spain, and, in his name and during his minority, the Queen Regent of the Kingdom: To all whom these presents shall come, know ye that the Cortes have decreed and we have sanctioned the following:

ARTICLE I. The system of government and the civil administration of the Island of Cuba shall be readjusted on the following bases:

BASIS I.

The laws of municipalities and of provinces now in force in the Island are hereby amended to the extent necessary for the following ends:

Provincial Assemblies and Municipalities.

The Council of Administration shall, upon the report of the Provincial Assemblies, decide all questions relating to the formation of municipalities, and to the determination of their boundaries.

The law of provinces is hereby amended as to the matters placed by these bases within the powers of the Council of Administration.

The Provincial Assembly shall decide all questions pertaining to the organization of Boards of Aldermen, to their election, to the qualification of the members and other similar questions.

Each Board of Aldermen shall elect one of its members as Mayor. The Governor General may remove a Mayor and appoint a new Mayor, but the new Mayor must be a member of the Board. In addition to their functions as executive officers of the Boards of Aldermen, the Mayors shall be the representatives and delegates of the Governor General.

Whenever the Governor General shall stay the resolutions of a municipal corporation* the matter shall be laid before the criminal courts, if the stay be due to misdemeanor com-

---

* See note page 53.

mitted by the corporation in connection with the resolutions, or laid before the Provincial Governor, upon the report of the Provincial Assembly, if the resolutions were stayed because they exceeded the powers of the Board, or because they infringed the law.

The Provincial Governors may stay the resolutions of the municipal corporation, and censure, warn, fine or suspend the members of the corporations when they exceed the limits of their powers.

Previous to removing Mayors or Aldermen, in the cases provided by law, the Governor General must give the Council of Administration a hearing upon the removal.

Every member of a municipal corporation who shall have presented or voted in favor of a resolution injurious to the rights of a citizen shall be under a liability, enforcible before the court having jurisdiction, to indemnify or make restitution to the injured party, the liability ceasing according to the rules of the Statute of Limitations.

Municipal Taxation. Each Board of Aldermen shall, in matters defined as within the exclusive municipal powers, have full freedom of action, agreeably with the observance of the law, and with the respect due to the rights of citizens. In order that the Boards of Aldermen and the guilds* may fix the amount of the taxes to cover the expenses of the municipality and may determine their nature and their distribution, in accordance with the preference of each municipality, the Boards of Aldermen and the guilds shall have all the powers necessary thereto, that is compatible with the system of taxation of the State.

The Provincial Assemblies may review the resolutions of municipal corporations relating to the preparation or alteration of their estimates of revenues and expenditures, and, while respecting their discretionary powers, shall see that no appropriation which exceeds the assets be allowed, and that arrears of previous years and payments ordered by courts having jurisdiction have the preference. The Governor General and the Provincial Governors shall in these matters have only the intervention necessary to insure the observance of the law and to prevent municipal taxation from impairing the sources of revenue of the State.

The annual accounts of each Mayor, inclusive of revenues

---

* For purposes of *taxation* the various trades are formed into guilds. Taxes on trades are apportioned among the guilds, whose officers fix the tax to be paid by each member according to the valuation of his business.

and expenditures, ordinary and extraordinary, shall be published in the municipality and audited and corrected by the Provincial Assembly, after hearing protests, and approved by the Provincial Governor if they do not exceed 100,000 pesetas, and by the Council of Administration if they exceed that sum. The Provincial Assemblies and the Council of Administration shall determine if any officials have incurred liabilities, except in the cases that come within the jurisdiction of the ordinary courts.

Appeals to the Council of Administration may be taken from the decisions of the Provincial Assemblies.

BASIS II.

The Council of Administration shall be organized as follows:

The Council.

The Governor General, or the acting Governor General, shall be President of the Council.

The Supreme Government shall appoint by Royal Decree fifteen of the Councilors.

The Council shall have a staff of secretaries, with the personnel necessary for the transaction of its affairs.

The office of Councilor shall be honorary and gratuitous.

For appointment as Councilor the appointee must have resided in the Island during the four years previous to appointment, and must have one of the following qualifications:

Councilors Appointed by the Crown.

To be or to have been President of a Chamber of Commerce, of the Economic Society of Friends of the Country, or of the Sugar Planters' Association.

To be or to have been Rector of the University, or Dean of the Corporation of Lawyers of a provincial capital for two years.

To have been for the four years previous to appointment one of the fifty principal taxpayers of the Island, paying taxes on real estate, on manufactures, on trade, or on licenses to practice a profession.

To have been a Senator of the Kingdom or a Representative to the Cortes in two or more legislatures.

To have been two or more times President of a Provincial Assembly of the Island; to have served for two or more terms of two years as member of the Provincial Executive Committee;* or to have been a Provincial Assemblyman eight years.

To have been for two or more terms of two years Mayor of a provincial capital.

To have been, until the proclamation of this act, member of the Administrative Council for two or more years.

The Council may, whenever it shall deem it expedient, summon to its deliberations, through the Governor General, any chief of department, but the latter shall not vote with the Council.

Councilors Elected by the People. To form the Council fifteen additional Councilors shall be elected by voters having the qualifications requisite to vote for Provincial Assemblymen.

The term of office shall be four years. The elections to fill vacated seats shall take place every two years, the Provinces of Havana, Pinar del Rio and Puerto Principe voting at one election, and the Provinces of Matanzas, Santa Clara and Santiago de Cuba voting at another.

The Province of Havana shall elect four Councilors; the Province of Santiago de Cuba shall elect three; and each of the other provinces shall elect two.

All the Councilors shall be elected at the same time: upon the establishment of this act, and after a total removal of the Council. Two years after the establishment of this act, or after a total removal of the Council, the Councilors from the first group of provinces above named shall vacate their seats, and their successors shall be elected.**

In ordinary cases the election shall take place at the same time as the elections for Provincial Assemblymen, the votes for Councilor and for Assemblyman being cast together.

The Council shall be the judge of the elections, returns and qualifications of the Councilors-elect and of the qualifications of the Councilors appointed by the Crown, and shall decide all questions concerning its own organization under the law.

BASIS III.

The Council of Administration shall resolve whatever it may deem proper for the management in the whole Island;

---

* Each of the six provinces of Cuba—like every other Spanish province—has a Provincial Assembly. The Assembly meets twice a year in sessions of about two weeks, and appoints from its members a Provincial Executive Committee (*comisión provincial*) to act during the intervals between the sessions.

** At the next election the Councilors elected for the second group of provinces would vacate their seats.

of public works, posts and telegraphs, railways and naviga- tion, agriculture, manufactures, trade, immigration and colonization, public instruction, charities and the health department, without prejudice to the supervision and to the powers inherent to the sovereignty of the nation, which are reserved by law to the Supreme Government.

Powers of the Council.

Each year it shall prepare and approve the estimates with sufficient appropriations for all those departments. It shall exercise the functions that the laws of provinces and of municipalities and other special laws shall attribute to it. It shall correct, and in the proper cases approve, the accounts of its revenues and expenditures, which accounts shall be rendered every year by the general management of the local administration,* and shall determine the liabilities therein incurred by officials.

The local revenues** shall consist of :

1. The proceeds of Crown lands and rents, and of the institutions whose financial management pertains to the Council.

Revenues.

2. The surcharges which, within the limits fixed by law, the council may add to the taxes imposed by the State.

It shall be the duty of the Governor General, as superior chief of the authorities of the Island, to carry out the resolutions of the Council.

For that purpose the general management of the local administration, as delegate of the Governor General, shall attend to the departments included in the local estimates and shall keep the books thereof and shall be responsible for the non-fulfillment of the laws and of the legitimate resolutions of the Council of Administration.

Whenever the Governor General may deem any resolution of the Council contrary to the law or to the general interests of the nation, he shall stay its execution, and shall of his own motion take such measures as the public needs—which would otherwise be neglected—may require, immediately submitting the matter to the Minister of the Colonies.

If any resolution of the Council unduly injures the rights of a citizen the Councilors who shall have contributed with their votes to the passage of the resolution shall be liable, before

* An office in charge of a superior official that under the Governor General act as the executive of the Council of Administration.

** Revenues of which the Council of Administration may dispose.

the courts having jurisdiction, to indemnify or make restitution to the injured party.

The Governor General, after hearing the Council of Authorities, may suspend the Council of Administration, or, without hearing the Council of Authorities, may suspend individual members of the Council of Administration as long as a number of Councilors sufficient to form a quorum remains:

1. When the Council or any one of its members transgresses the limits of its legitimate powers, and impairs the authority of the Governor General or the judicial authority, or threatens to disturb the public peace.

2. For a misdemeanor.

In the first case the Governor General shall immediately inform the Supreme Government of the suspension, so that the latter may either set it aside or, through a resolution adopted by the Council of Ministers within two months, decree the removal. If at the expiration of the two months the suspension has not been acted upon, it shall, as a matter of right, be deemed set aside.

In the second case, the matter shall come before the court having jurisdiction, which shall be the full Supreme Court of Havana, and its decision therein shall be final. In other cases the accused may appeal.

The Council shall have a hearing:

1. Upon the general estimates of expenditures and revenues of the Island, which estimates, prepared by the Finance Department of the Island, shall be submitted yearly, together with the changes suggested by the Council, during the month of March, or earlier, to the Minister of the Colonies.

Although the Supreme Government may have varied the estimates before submitting them to the Cortes for appropriations to meet the expenses of the departments and the general obligations of the state, it shall always submit with them, for purposes of information, the changes suggested by the council.

2. Upon the general accounts, which the Finance Department of the Island must without fail submit annually within the six months following the end of the fiscal year, and which shall include the revenues collected and the expenditures liquidated.

3. Upon the matters pertaining to the patronage* of the Indies.

4. Upon the decisions of Provincial Governors which shall come on appeal before the Governor General.

5. Upon the removals or suspensions of Mayors and Aldermen.

6. Upon other matters of a general nature.

The Governor General may demand of the Council the reports he may desire.

The Council shall meet in ordinary sessions at stated intervals, and in extraordinary session whenever the Governor General may summon it.

BASIS IV.

The Governor General shall be the representative of the National Government in the Island of Cuba. He shall as vice-royal patron exercise the powers inherent to the patronage of the Indies. He shall be the Commander-in-Chief of the Army and Navy stationed on the Island. He shall be the delegate of the Ministers of the Colonies, of State, of War and of the Navy. All the other authorities of the Island shall be his subordinates. He shall be appointed and removed by the President of the Council of Ministers, with the assent of the Council.

Powers and Duties of the Governor General.

In addition to the other functions which pertain to him by law or by special delegation of the Government it shall be his duty:

To proclaim, execute and cause to be executed, on the Island, the laws, decrees, treaties, international conventions and other mandates that emanate from the legislature.

To proclaim, execute and cause to be executed the decrees, Royal orders, and other mandates that emanate from

---

* In England when lords of manors first built and endowed churches on their lands they had the right of nominating clergymen (provided they were canonically qualified) to officiate in them. This right is the "patronage" (*jus patronatus*). The Bulls of Alexander VI. in 1493 and of Julius II. in 1508 granted the Crown of Spain the patronage of the Indies (New World). It includes not only the right of presentation to the churches and monasteries built and endowed by the Crown, but other rights so extensive that the author speaks of the Kings of Spain as the "born delegates of the Holy See and apostolic vicar-generals in the Indies."—*Translator's Note.*

the executive, and which the Ministers, whose delegate he is, may communicate to him.

To suspend the proclamation and execution of resolutions of His Majesty's Government, when in his judgment such resolutions might prove injurious to the general interests of the nation or to the special interests of Island, informing the Minister concerned of the suspension, and of the reason therefor, in the speediest manner possible.

To superintend and inspect all the departments of the public service.

To communicate directly upon foreign affairs with the representatives, diplomatic agents and consuls of Spain in the Americas.

To suspend, after consultation with the Council of Authorities, the execution of a sentence of death, whenever the gravity of the circumstances may require it, and the urgency of the case be such that there is no opportunity to apply to His Majesty for pardon.

To suspend, after consultation with the same Council, and on his own responsibility, whenever extraordinary circumstances prevent previous communication with the Supreme Government, the constitutional rights expressed in Articles IV., V., VI. and IX., and Sections 1, 2 and 3 of Article XIII. of the Constitution of the State, and to apply the Riot Act.

It shall also be the duty of the Governor General as head of the civil administration:

To keep each department of the administration within the limits of its powers.

To devise the general rules necessary for the execution of the laws and regulations, submitting them to the Minister of the Colonies.

To conform strictly to the regulations and orders devised by the Supreme Government for the due execution of the laws.

To determine the penal institutions in which sentences are to be served, to order the incarceration therein of convicts, and to designate the jail liberties when the courts order confinement therein.

To suspend any public official whose appointment pertains to the Supreme Government, giving the Government immediate notice of the suspension, with the reasons therefor, and to fill *pro tempore* the vacancy in accordance with the regulations now in force.

To act as intermediary between the Ministers, whose delegate he is, and all the authorities of the Island.

The Council of Authorities shall consist of the following members: The Bishop of Havana or the Reverend the Archbishop of Santiago de Cuba, if the latter be present; the Commander of the Naval Station, the Military Governor, the presiding justice of the Supreme Court of Havana, the Attorney-General, the head of the Department of Finances, and the director of local administration.

The resolutions of this Council shall be drawn up in duplicate and one of the copies shall be sent to the Minister of the Colonies. They are not binding upon the Governor General. All his acts must be upon his own responsibility.

The Governor General shall not surrender his office nor absent himself from the Island without the express order of the Supreme Government.

In case of vacancy, absence or inability the Military Governor shall be his substitute, and in default of the latter the Commander of the Naval Station, until the Supreme Government appoints a *pro tempore* Governor General.

The criminal part of the Supreme Court at Madrid shall have the sole jurisdiction over the Governor General for infractions of the Penal Code. Charges of maladministration against the Governor General shall be brought before the Council of Ministers.

The Governor General shall not amend nor revoke his own decisions when they: have been confirmed by the Supreme Government; or have vested rights; or have served as the basis of a judgment of a court, or of the adjudication of a mixed juridical administrative tribunal; or when he bases his decision upon the limitations of his powers.

BASIS V.

The civil and financial administration of the Island, under the supervision of the Governor General, shall be organized in accordance with the following rules:

The Governor General with his staff of secretaries, which shall be under the direction of a chief of department, shall attend directly to matters of government, the patronage of the Indies, conflicts of jurisdiction, public peace, foreign affairs, jails, penitentiaries, statistics, personnel of the departments, communication between all the authorities of the Island and the Supreme Government, and all the other matters that are unassigned.

The Finance Department, which shall be under the charge of a superior chief of department, shall attend to the whole management of the finances; it shall keep the books, and audit and submit the accounts of the estimates of the State on the Island.

The provincial administrative sections shall be under the direct control of the Finance Department, without prejudice to the supervision that the Governor General may delegate in fixed cases to the Provincial Governor.

The general management of local administration, under the charge of a superior chief of administration, shall attend to the departments that shall be supported with the appropriations made by the Council of Administration; it shall keep the books, and audit and submit the annual accounts of the estimates of the Council and of the municipalities, and shall enforce the resolutions of the Council of Administration.

The personnel of the offices and the methods for the transaction of affairs shall be adapted to the object of obtaining the greatest simplicity in the transaction of affairs and in fixing official responsibility.

The rules of law shall determine the cases in which a right is vested through the decision of a superior official in a matter that, in accordance with this basis, falls within his jurisdiction, so that an action before the mixed juridical-administrative tribunal may lie.

Nevertheless the injured party may at any time bring a complaint before the Governor General in matters which concern the Finance Department and the general management of local administration, and also before the Minister of the Colonies in any matter that concerns the administration or the government of the Island; but the complaint shall not interrupt the administrative process, nor the legal procedure, nor the course of the action before the mixed juridical-administrative tribunal.

The Governor General and the Minister of the Colonies, when using their powers of supervision, either on their own initiative or owing to a complaint, shall refrain from interrupting the ordinary course of affairs, as long as there be no necessity of taking measures to remedy or prevent irreparable damage, before the final decision of the competent authority. ———

ARTICLE II.*

Provincial Elections. ARTICLE III. The system of election and the division of the provinces into districts for the provincial elections shall be

---

* Article II. of this act refers exclusively to Porto Rico. Article III. refers both to Cuba and to Porto Rico.

modified by the Government, in order to enable minorities in both Cuba and Porto Rico to have representation in the municipalities and in the Provincial Assemblies, and in Cuba in the Council of Administration of Cuba, and in order to apply to the election of Aldermen, Provincial Assemblymen and Councilors of Administration—in so far as the qualifications of voters and the annual formation and rectification of the registration lists are concerned—the provisions of the Royal Decree of December 27, 1892, upon the reform of the electoral law for the election of representatives to the Cortes, Articles XIV., XV. and XVI. of the said Royal Decree shall be extended to all classes of elections.

For all electoral purposes the taxes imposed by the Council of Administration in Cuba, and by the Provincial Assembly in Porto Rico, by virtue of the new powers granted to them by this act, shall be computed as if imposed by the State.

ADDITIONAL ARTICLE.

The Government shall render to the Cortes an account of the use it makes of the powers hereby granted to it.

TRANSITIONAL PROVISIONS.

1. The Councilors of Administration elected in the Island of Cuba upon the proclamation of this act shall stay in office until the first election for Provincial Assemblymen that happens after two years have passed since the first election of the Council.

2. The rectification, according to the methods that shall be established under Article III. of this act, of the registration lists for the election of Aldermen and of Provincial Assemblymen in both Cuba and Porto Rico, and of Councilors of Administration in Cuba, shall commence from the time of the proclamation of this act.

The Minister for the Colonies shall ordain, by Royal Decree, the necessary measures, and shall fix the time for the various operations of the rectification, so that it may be finished before any election take place to establish the Council of Administration in Cuba or to fill the seats of members of municipal corporations whose terms have expired.

The election for the latter purpose shall under no circumstances be postponed, except in the case of the Boards of Aldermen,* which, in this present year, and if the Supreme

* Municipal corporations in Cuba, as in the Peninsula, have a Board of Aldermen (*ayuntamiento*) and a Municipal Council (*junta municipal*).

Government deem it necessary, may be postponed until the first fortnight of next June.

In subsequent years the rectification shall take place in the manner provided by the Royal Decree of December 27, 1892, referred to in Article III. of this act.

Therefore:

We order all the courts, justices, chiefs, governors and other authorities, civil, military and ecclesiastical, of whatsoever class or dignity, to keep, and cause to be kept, fulfill and execute this act in all its parts.

Given in the Palace, March 15, 1895.

I, THE QUEEN REGENT.

The Minister for the Colonies.

BUENAVENTURA ABARZUZA.

www.ingramcontent.com/pod-product-compliance
Lightning Source LLC
Chambersburg PA
CBHW030721110426
42739CB00030B/1063